Private

RockStar Teenage Girl

*SELF and Confidence Building
for Tween & Teenage Girls*

Nordica Francis

This book is dedicated to my parents,
Claude and Angela Francis,
both teachers, whose life's work it
was to educate young and
old – at different times, at various levels,
and in several disciplines.
They were my greatest role models.

I love you Mom and Dad.

Nordica

Dear Mom and Dad of a Tween or Teenage Girl:

This book is written especially with your tween or teenage daughter in mind; I was once at her age and stage in life. I've worked with girls her age for close to 30 years and I adore them. I also see their struggles. They have anxieties about fitting in, being cool, being liked by boys, and being accepted for who they are. Running right alongside these concerns, are expectations to excel in school, please their parents, and establish their autonomy. At the same time, their bodies are changing, and they're figuring out who they are and who they want to be eventually.

It's a delicate balancing act. Unfortunately, girls' struggles with this balancing act can result in a lack of self-esteem or self-confidence, failure in school, anxiety, depression, and in some cases, even self-injurious behavior.

This book contains 14 principles designed to help tween and teenage girls navigate their middle and high school years with reduced stress and increased happiness and success. It is a given that they must work at their highest potential level to succeed academically. In addition to that principal endeavor, however, they must face social challenges and all of the difficulties associated with their tween and teenage years, and growing into womanhood. The book is meant to help girls build a strong sense of themselves, and develop esteem and confidence levels that would allow them to adopt healthy lifestyles, have great success in the endeavors they undertake, and enjoy happiness throughout their lives.

It is also meant to help you help them. Of course, they can read the book themselves; I've kept the language simple and direct. However, it would be nice if you read it, too, so that some of the principles could be discussed during quality time that you spend together.

I hope that both you and she will immensely enjoy reading it.

Sincerely,

Nordica Francis

Table of Contents

TABLE OF CONTENTS

ACKNOWLEDGEMENTS

My first acknowledgment, of course, is to God for the numerous blessings he has bestowed upon me throughout my life; blessings of family, friends, good health, happiness, and inspiration. Inspiration has come through my parents, first and foremost, and through my interactions with teachers and mentors, and other adults in my childhood. Inspiration has also come through the many great authors that I have read, whether they dealt with practical matters or spiritual matters; not that the two are at any time mutually exclusive. God has also given me abundant strength and much courage.

I have needed those, as well, in difficult times.

If I start acknowledging people by name I could get myself into serious trouble, as I'm bound to miss someone who is very important in my life. For this reason, I simply acknowledge the people I interact with on a daily or almost daily basis. They are the ones I spend holidays with, or with whom I crack up in hysterical girlish laughter. Then there are the ones to whom I run for solace and advice, or call up just to hear myself think out loud. They're part of the everyday fabric of my life, and they and I know quite well who they are.

Yes, mine is a simple life. I'm not being inspired daily by kings and presidents, or government officials, or even CEOs of companies. Mine is an everyday life of family, friends, colleagues, cousins, nieces and nephews. Nieces and nephews that came through my brothers, as well as those I've "stolen". The stolen ones came to me through friends male and female. Every time a friend of mine gave birth, I automatically became an aunt. I'm sure that this experience is pretty common, but I mention it because it means the world to me.

I've also been blessed to have taught and interacted with thousands of children over the course of thirty years working in schools. They, too, have enriched my life in countless ways. Say what you want about high-profile jobs, nothing beats the experience of a smile from a grateful child, or a "light bulb" moment on the face of a student who took a while to "get it". One of the special experiences, early in my teaching career, was a class of second graders bringing me large bouquets of those little yellow weeds that pop up all over the place at the beginning of springtime. You should just see the excitement on their faces as they presented these 'flowers' to their teacher. And yes. I put them in a coffee mug with water immediately, and the next day brought in a little vase in which to proudly display them on my desk. Simple joy!

The love and support and encouragement of all these people weaving their lives through mine every day bring me simple joy. Thanks to all of them. A million thanks!

PREFACE

The Reason for the Work

I decided to do this book for a very simple reason, and the reason is this:

I see the anguish of teenage girls every day as they embark on the road to womanhood, strive to discover who they are while they fit in with a clique, or even just try to gain the respect of an "In group". They may not, in many cases, want to be a member of an "In group", believing right from the start that they wouldn't quite fit in, but they do want to be allowed to be who they are without getting the overhaul as they approach a group, being constantly criticized or judged, or being the butt of cruel jokes and/or the object of malicious gossip. A girl's need to belong and to be accepted by her peers is a sub life that runs concurrently with her regular, daily life as a tween or teenage girl.

I am not saying here that every teenage girl faces the issues mentioned above. There are girls who just seem to have been born confident and self-sufficient people, but for a vast number of teenage girls, these situations become major issues. I am also not saying that teenage boys do not face some of these problems as well, but teenage girls are the ones who seem to suffer most, or suffer most overtly from them. Something in the nature of boys allows them to be more resilient in the face of competition, rejection, and criticism than girls are, and they seem to be just fine. On the other hand, girls develop self-esteem and confidence issues as a result of the same competition, rejection, and criticism; it's something I see on an up close and personal level every day. Maybe at this point, it would be appropriate to establish how I get to see these problems on an up close and personal level every day, and how I've come to understand what goes on in the minds and psyches of teenage girls. Let me say, also, that being a woman now, means that I was once a teenage girl. Ha!

I first earned a Bachelor's Degree in Psychology with a minor in Human Relations, and began my career in education as a classroom teacher in the New York City Public School System. During that time, I studied for and earned a Master's Degree in Educational Administration and Supervision. After many years of teaching and working closely with both boys and girls in that 11 to 18 age range, I returned to school and did postgraduate work to become a Learning Disabilities Teacher Consultant. I currently work in one of New Jersey State's largest public school districts as a learning consultant. All told, my experience working with tween and teenage girls spans a period of almost 30 years, as of the writing date of this book.

In addition to my duties of teaching, observing, speaking to, and working with tween and teenage girls in their instructional environments on a daily basis, I screen them for learning disabilities if they are referred for evaluation, and then based on the results of the evaluation, must follow up with writing an Individualized Education Program for each student.

I also do case management of students. At this level, parents and teachers are drawn into the equation, and this is where issues other than those that are academic in nature rise to the surface and must be resolved. Some of these issues might indeed be having a direct, and usually negative, impact on the student's ability to do her best academic work and achieve success at her highest potential level.

Let me make it clear that my experience with these issues is not solely related to students with special needs. I work with girls on a very wide spectrum of cognitive ability. I see these issues arising for very many pre-teen and teenage girls, seemingly a particularly vulnerable group, regardless of classification, cognitive ability, or socio-economic background. While these problems typically begin to manifest for girls during their middle and/or high school years, they invariably spill into their outside lives, and severe difficulties can develop in their social arena, as well as in their later educational and working careers.

The difficulties of tween and teenage girls discussed in this book frequently result in poor self-image, low self-esteem, and impoverished confidence levels that can last well into adulthood and negatively impact later success. Again, boys also have some of the negative and anxiety-causing experiences that girls have, but somehow they have been observed to handle them differently. They rarely end up in a case manager's or counselor's office with tremulous hands, streams of tears, vomiting, depressed expressions, cuts on their bodies, or suicidal ideation. They also rarely have failing grades in the face of high cognitive ability, due to the fact that they are not accepted by the cool clique, or because the girl they like doesn't like them back. It's very different for girls.

Let's take a look at a short list of the effects of being a tween or teenage girl who is left out of the cool clique, or who experiences rejection, competition, and criticism on a consistent basis. To name a few, they are: feeling victimized, feeling bullied psychologically and emotionally, feeling left out or shunned; feeling undeserving, feeling unworthy, feeling mistreated, loathed, not smart enough, not pretty enough, not cool enough, not attractive enough to others; just generally feeling not good enough. What are the problems that can result from these feelings of inferiority or inadequacy?

To scratch the surface: substandard academic achievement and functional performance in school, self-destructive or self-injurious behaviors like cutting themselves, promiscuity, too-early pregnancy and motherhood, drug and alcohol abuse, severe depression, eating disorders, and in many cases, suicidal ideation. These problems can range in severity from something simple that requires small group counseling by the school's guidance counselor to much more serious issues that require the clinical expertise and help of a mental health professional.

While this book does not attempt to give clinical advice, or presume to replace the help that can be had from a mental health professional, it is a tool that tween and teenage girls can use to empower themselves with high self-esteem and confidence; self-esteem and confidence that would allow them to adopt healthy lifestyles, have success with the endeavors they undertake, and be generally happier in their lives. The book will also help parents, grandparents, teachers, and other adults to bring the struggles of tween and teenage girls into clear view, and provide a framework within which to begin hearing, acknowledging, understanding, and assisting them during this important period of growing into womanhood.

INTRODUCTION

The work lays out fourteen principles, presented in two books: A book of seven personal principles and a book of seven spiritual principles. The principles are stated in the first person so that they can be repeated as affirmations, if needed.

The first seven of the fourteen principles are called Personal Principles, and girls will relate to them on an everyday, practical, common sense level. The second seven of these principles will move to that higher ground of caring for the spirit, and are called Spiritual Principles, because all human beings are in the first place spiritual beings. What creates much of the unhappiness and anguish that is experienced in everyday life is the fact that many false notions about ourselves have been given to us, which we have come to believe, and now use as a point from which to operate. These inaccurate ideas are regarded as truth, and from that viewpoint, experiences are generated in our lives which substantiate the negative notions. Negative experiences manifest themselves as a result of negative beliefs. These all begin on an intangible plane, with a belief system that negates who we are as divine beings.

It is for this reason that the book provides spiritual principles as well; ones that teenage girls can adopt and live by. These principles have nothing to do with religion. They are principles that are meant to replace the negative notions and ideas that were implanted in the psyche at some point, and now serve as truth, directing and controlling the lives of tween or teenage girls. There needs to be a switching out of the old beliefs that create limitation for new ones that create possibilities, as well as the manifestation of all that is desired and deserved.

While the language used is simple and direct, the Spiritual Principles have their roots in teachings usually reserved for adults who are attempting to identify their own issues of poor self-image, low confidence levels, failure at some undertakings in their lives (no one fails at everything), and who are seeking a way to manifest their full potential and live their best life.

This book will prove to be an invaluable addition to the library of every tween and teenage girl.

RockStar
Teenage Girl

*SELF and Confidence Building
for Tween & Teenage Girls*

Book 1
7 Personal Principles

My FIRST Principle

I Am Good Enough Exactly The Way I Am.

*It really doesn't matter what
anyone says or thinks about me.
I know that I'm good enough, and the fact that
I was born and am alive in the world,
makes me **automatically worthy**.
I Love Myself.*

WORTHY: valuable, admirable, commendable, precious

It's easy to develop self-doubt, especially in your pre-teen and teenage years. Everything seems to be going well, and suddenly things change. Now you're beginning to be concerned with your body, the way you look to others, and what they might be thinking about you. We say what they *might* be thinking, because much of the time no one has shared exactly what they're thinking.

3

You're mostly interpreting people's behavior toward you based on the way that you feel about yourself.

If you don't feel pretty enough, or think you're not fashionable enough, or not popular enough, you may think that others feel the same way about you. It isn't necessarily so. That is not to say your feelings should be discounted. **If you feel it, it's real to you, and therefore very important.**

However, here's a fact that you might not have considered: Most people are so self-centered, and their focus is so much on themselves, they might not be thinking of you at all. This is especially true of the arrogant, popular types who think that the world revolves around them.

It's usually just all about *their* hair, and *their* makeup, and all about

"When you accept and love yourself exactly as you are, it shows, and everyone else accepts the fact that you're good enough exactly as you are."

their outfits and *their* attractiveness to others. They're showing some kind of confidence in themselves, although sometimes it smacks of arrogance, that you are not allowing yourself to feel about *your* self and who *you* are.

The trick is to boost your own self-confidence. When you know who you are and like yourself enough, it shows.

If your style of dress is different, it's uniquely you. If you think you want the things others have, examine your own situation. Are these the things that you or your family can afford to spend money on right now? Talk to your parents honestly. You might have to wait a little while to get that popular item, or fashionable outfit, or designer purse. You might have to save a little of your allowance each time you get one, in order to buy that item yourself.

Believe it or not, parents understand about girls growing up and their need to fit in. They won't intentionally make you wear ugly clothes or be unpopular. Your attitude is very important here. *If you accept yourself, and* **enjoy the things you do have**, *instead of constantly wishing for the things you don't have, that peace and contentment with yourself will show through.*

An important principle of happiness is to focus on the best aspects of yourself, not your external appearance.

In another principle of this book, we'll talk about radiating beauty from the inside out. You will have the self-confidence that other girls - and boys - find very attractive. Be careful, though, not to feign self-confidence. It must truly reside *in* you; you must know what the wonderful things about yourself are and believe in them, see them as gifts, as qualities that make you special, and worthy, and good enough. When you know these things about yourself, there is no need to post your picture on YouTube asking the world: *"Am I pretty?"*

How do you achieve this self-confidence? This is a great question and one you might want to answer for yourself, as it will serve you for your entire life.

Take some time to sit quietly by yourself and list the things you like about yourself. Make a written list; it helps to be able to see your special qualities in writing. Read the list often. Internalize it. Know, and believe in your heart, that you have these wonderful qualities. Feel them deep inside yourself.

What are you good at? What are you passionate about? Start your list with, "This is what is really great about me" or "This is what I truly love about me". Here are some examples of questions to help you get started:

- Are you a good listener when others need your attention?
- Are you kind to others?
- Do you have a great sense of humor?
- Do you care about less fortunate people?
- Will you protect children who are younger than yourself?
- Do you look out for the well-being of your younger siblings or cousins?

- Do you find it easy to share?

- Do you care about justice and fairness?

- In school, do you always make an effort at doing your best academic work?

- Do you have a beautiful voice for singing, or a talent for acting?

- Do you find that you write well and creatively?

- Do you have a knack for working with numbers?

- Are you very good at building things, or drawing, or at a particular sport?

This does not have to be a long list. It can be a list of just two or three things that you *truly love* about yourself. You might want to put that list in a place where you can see it every day. Put a copy of it by your bedside so you see it first thing in the morning and last thing at night, in a journal, or on your mirror. If you share a bedroom or bathroom and would rather keep it private, you can carry it on your person—tucked away in your purse, pocket, or the inside cover of a binder that you access during the course of the school day; even on the inside of your locker door. You can have it in as many places as you like.

The important thing is that your list is readily visible to you.
When something happens that shakes your confidence a little, you have your instant reminder of what you love about yourself. All you have to do is read it and

you'll remember who you are. After a while, you won't even have to read the list, just seeing it will be enough to remind you of your self-love.

Somehow, the way you feel about yourself is transmitted to others, and in large part, determines the way they treat you. Understand, however, that there will be some people who do not like the fact that you know who you are. They might resent the fact that you do not depend on them or their compliments to feel good about yourself, and might not want to be friends with you.

That's okay. **People who cannot or would not want you to be your best self should not be in your circle of friends anyway.** It would be enough to be cordial and polite to them; you'll probably still have to interact with them in your cooperative learning groups or other school and community activities. However, they do not have to be your close friends.

It is important to surround yourself with people who are supportive of your efforts at becoming a better student, or a better person. These are friends who will be complimentary when you deserve a compliment, will be honest, but speak kindly to you if they must bring something to your attention that they think is wrong, and who will be always respectful of your right to be who you are.

Parents and teachers, too, are usually very good support systems for nurturing and bringing out the best qualities that you possess. If you have a little trouble sharing with your parents (for some teenagers, this is just a difficult thing to do), find a teacher or school counselor that you can trust; one who will willingly give you some of his or her time, will keep your confidences (as long as you are not posing a danger to yourself or anyone else), and encourage you to achieve your goals. He or she might even help you get a clearer vision of what you want for yourself, and help you to set and achieve some of those goals.

Finally, create a mantra for yourself; something you can always say to yourself that will instantly boost your self-confidence and remind you that you're good enough, exactly the way you are.

* * *

All the Great Things about Me!

What do I totally love about myself?

* ★ Smart
* ★ atethic athletic
* ★ animal lover

What do I feel confident about?

* ★ being who I am
* ★ caring about others
* ★ helping animals/ppl.

How do I know that I am good enough exactly the way I am?

* ★ my skills
* ★ my history
* ★ ppl around me say so

Here's more great stuff that I love about myself!

★ into boys a lot

★ anime lover

★ Video gamer

★ sense of humor

What does your magic look like?
What do you think is special
about you?

Growing Better from the Inside Out!

Here are some additional attributes that I now possess and / or want to develop, and how they will help me:

Attribute	How it will help me:
Honesty	trust others
Integrity	
Sincerity	
Compassion	care others
Patience	take time

My SECOND Principle

I Am Unique. I Do Not Compare Myself with Others

*I have abilities and talents that
are different from anyone else's.
I can be a better ME than I can be anyone else.
I'll always be myself,
and have full confidence in my ability to
succeed at whatever I want to do.*

UNIQUE: distinctive, irreplaceable, exceptional, only one of its kind

Let me tell you a true story about having unique talents and great self-confidence. It happened in the spring of 2012 and involved a tween girl, a teenage girl, and a mom, so you definitely can relate to it.

There is a popular television show called *Shark Tank* on which people appear with their inventions, and ask the investors (the sharks) to invest money to help them launch their product or make their businesses a success, in exchange for a small part of their company.

There is a great episode of *Shark Tank* about a teenage girl, Maddie, now fifteen, who started making magnets for her locker from bottle caps at the age of ten. She painted a design on the inside of the bottle cap and glued a magnet to the back of it. These magnets she later made into necklaces by attaching cords to them. Her friends at school went crazy for the item, and Mattie introduced the necklaces to local stores which sold out of them within hours. That was the start of her jewelry business, and it did so well that she enlisted the help of her ten-year-old sister, Margot, and her mom. Together, they formed a company called M3 Girl Designs (M3 stands for Maddie, Margot and Mom), and these girls are now millionaires. They have had over 5 million dollars in sales in the last five years. That's $5,000,000.00; roughly a million dollars a year. Not bad for a ten and a fifteen year old! They are millionaires and they don't even have a license to drive! Their jewelry is now in stores all across the nation.

The girls went to *Shark Tank* to ask for three hundred thousand dollars to take their business global. Four out of five investors (sharks) wanted to be in on the deal.

Did the girls take the first offer they got? **No way**. They negotiated back and forth with the sharks until they got exactly the financial deal they wanted, PLUS season tickets to the basketball games of the Dallas Mavericks, and use of the team owner's private suite for their family and friends added into the bargain. You see, one of the sharks was Mark Cuban who owns the Dallas Mavericks. Don't for one moment think that Mom was the one speaking for them. It was Maddie, the president of the company, the 15 year-old, who was the chief negotiator along with her little sister Margot, the vice president. The sharks were *very* impressed. They could not believe their ears and eyes, and were only too happy to be part of a successful company started by a tween and a teenage girl. Although four of the sharks wanted to be in on the deal, the girls wanted only three, and they had no qualms about eliminating one of them. Their story made national headlines.

I tell this true story to make the point about **unique talent**. Who would think of painting a design into a bottle cap, attaching a magnet to the back so it snaps on and off, then attaching it to a cord and making a necklace that sells like hot cakes? Maddie.

What bright idea do *you* have? It's not the snap cap jewelry idea, but you bet there's something smart in that brain of yours. Do you now think that you have to go out and start a company that nets a million dollars a year? No. Not that you can't, but that is not the point being made here. Think about **your own** unique talent. What do you do for hours and enjoy so much that time seems to fly by? That's usually a good clue. You might not necessarily come up with an invention, but you can certainly excel at whatever your talent is. It can be art, cooking, writing, sports, crochet, knitting, pottery, dance, or singing. Are you good at decorating, or designing clothing? Are you usually the one in charge of directing the school play or building the scenery for the backdrop? What are you good at? You tell me! Better still, you tell the world!!

> *"Do yourself an enormous favor.*
> *Don't try to be somebody you "ain't."*
> **Bob Beaudine,** *U.S. Sports/Entertainment*
> *Search Executive*

Don't ever dismiss your ideas, or think they are silly. Don't say "oh, lots of people draw." You have your own unique touch; your own unique eye. Start small. Improve. Go from there. Learn everything you can about anything you can. Talk to grownups. Ask about the things they do. Get new ideas. Read about everything that interests you.

When the Sharks asked Maddie what her margin was, she didn't turn to her mother for the answer. She didn't ask them what they meant, or say that she didn't understand the question. Immediately she was able to tell them what it cost her to make a necklace and how much it sold for. She knew what a margin was. She knew her business **and** her craft.

If you're interested in one particular thing, learn everything you can about it. Learn all the terms, all of the vocabulary, all the sources and resources. Talk to people you can learn from, or who can help you. If you haven't yet identified something you want to do or excel at, do not be discouraged. It means that your field of possibilities is still wide open. There is no limit to the possibilities for success with your unique talent - and *you do have a unique talent.* It is just a matter of identifying it. **Find it! Go for it! Good Luck!**

* * *

Growing Better from the Inside Out!

What are my unique talents?

being good goalie soccer

dance with my hand

take care of animal

What am I engaged in when time seems to fly?

My Action Steps for Developing My Talent(s):

_____

_____

_____

_____

_____

_____

_____

_____

_____

_____

_____

_____

_____

_____

_____

_____

_____

_____

_____

_____

_____

_____

_____

_____

* * *

My THIRD Principle

I Can Say NO to Negative Behaviors and Not Worry That My Friends Won't Like Me or Accept Me. I Set My Own Standards

*Peer pressure does not work with me.
I will not agree to anything that makes
me uncomfortable, or do anything that
I think is wrong for me.*

STANDARDS: principles, norms, values

You are a daughter, sister, aunt, niece, or student at this particular time in your life. What this means is that you have some responsibility to others. While you do indeed possess your own will, and can say No, there are rules and expectations with which you must comply within your family and within your school.

What you CAN say No to, is peer pressure that suggests you do the wrong thing, or do something that is wrong for you. When friends ask you to smoke or drink, or stay out past your curfew, to engage in sexual behavior, or to join in bullying, YOU CAN SAY NO. You can say No and not worry that they won't like or accept you because you made the right decision for yourself. This is sometimes difficult to do because you don't want to feel different or left out. It's okay.

One of the great dangers faced by young girls is coercion by boys. Boys force girls who are not ready, and who say clearly that they are not ready, to engage in sexual intercourse with them. They are somehow able to convince them that everything will be fine, and teenage pregnancy is the result. A Liz Claiborne, Inc. study conducted by *Teenage Research Unlimited* revealed that one in four girls who have been in relationships have been pressured to perform oral sex or engage in intercourse.

A big No-No for girls (for everyone, but especially for young girls) is the new fad known as *Sexting.* This is when girls send lewd or naked pictures of themselves over the internet to their boyfriends, or have suggestive conversations with them on the phone. Just about everyone has a smart phone now, and texts and pictures are easily sent over the internet and shared with everyone else.

Sometimes boys will save these pictures and use them as a bargaining tool to get girls to engage in sexual acts with them. They threaten to post the picture on *Face-Book* or other social media if the girls do not let them have their way. Out of fear of shame, disgrace, and scandalous rumors, the girl goes along with the boy's wishes, even if in her heart of hearts she knows this is the last thing that she wants to do. Please know, too, that oral sex is also sex, and very dangerous for you. Girls have shared that they thought this was okay since they didn't go "all the way".

When faced with difficult choices, think quickly about the standards you've set for yourself:

- I will carry myself in a ladylike manner.

- I will use clean language always.

- I will refrain from acts of vulgarity or lewdness (sexting; posting naked photos of myself on the Internet).

- I will not bully or stand idly by when someone is being bullied.

- I will state my position and stand up for myself.

- I will not use drugs because my friends want me to do so.

- I will not go against my own values for fear of being left out, or not fitting in.

- I will feel confident in making the right choices and decisions for myself.

- **I will not be forced to have sexual intercourse before I am old enough, or psychologically and emotionally ready.**

This last decision is of critical importance given the large number of teenage pregnancies in the United States. At this time, the USA is said to top teenage pregnancy and abortion in the world in its numbers.

It is a good idea, at this young and vulnerable age, to date in groups or in pairs. Ask another couple to join you and your boyfriend on a date. Ask him to pick you up at your parents' home and let him know that your parents expect you back by a certain time. You put yourself in much less danger when your parents are aware of your whereabouts and know who your friends are. It is less dangerous for you when there are others around on your date, especially if you've already had glimpses of things you don't like in your boyfriend's character or behavior.

Be self-respecting. Do not worry that if you don't go along with your boyfriend's wishes or threats, he will leave you for someone else. A boy who truly loves you will not put you in that position, or force you to make that choice. At some point, someone will come along who appreciates the fact that you have good values, are able to set boundaries, and have high self-esteem and self-respect. He will know that you're a lady, and would treat you as such.

When the ordeal or conflicting situation has passed, your self-esteem will be higher, and your confidence will be stronger, because you were wise enough, disciplined enough, and brave enough to make the choices and decisions that were right for you.

* * *

Growing Better from the Inside Out!

What will I strive for in the way I live my life?

_____

_____

_____

_____

_____

My FOURTH Principle

I Am Confident. I'm Not Afraid to Ask for What I Want. I Set Boundaries for Myself. I Teach Others How to Treat Me.

I never settle for less than I really want;
I'm not afraid to ask for it. I know that I deserve
the very best. I set boundaries in
my interactions with others so that
no one takes advantage of me.
I teach others how to treat me.

CONFIDENCE: self-assurance, poise, certainty, assertion, coolness

You must do it! You must ask for what you want. There's no getting around this. No one is going to read your mind. No one is just going to imagine what you might want and hand it to you, or give it to you because they think you deserve it. They might know that you deserve it, but still not offer it, or volunteer to let you have it. We're not referring to asking for items. We're talking about asking for everything else. For example, if there's an opportunity available that you know you really want, **you must drum up your courage and confidence and ask for it.**

If you need help to take the next step with something you want to pursue, you must ask for that help. If you need specific information about something you're interested in, but know very little about, you must seek out the professionals in that field and *ask* for that information…. *ask, ask, ask.* No. You're not being a nuisance. The thing is this: If the opportunity is present, it means that it's there to help you. Most of the time the people we can get help from are already part of our lives, or will show up. They can either help you directly, or find you the help you need, but *you do need to ask.*

When you ask, you need to be very specific about what you want. Don't tell a potential employer that you just want a summer job. Before you go in for that interview or complete that application, learn as much as possible about the company, and let the prospective employer know specifically what you'd like to do in that company or place of work.

Say you'd like a summer stint at your local library. Are you volunteering your time because you're interested in becoming a librarian and would give up some free time to learn about the system by which books are arranged? Do you want to become familiar with various genres? Would you like to work at the checkout counter for a chance to interact with people and make contact with folks who could probably be beneficial to you in another area of your life?

Do you want to be responsible for putting books back in their respective places once they've been returned, and get a salary for that job? Would you rather work in the children's section so you could mentor or tutor a younger child, and in that way give back to your community? Getting exactly what you want doesn't always come easy; it might take several tries, but the first step to your success is this:

Know exactly what you want, and don't let a fear of failure or rejection hold you back.

There are three key reasons why people don't get what they want, and end up settling for less (*and if they're not careful, this could happen over an entire lifetime***).**

1) They're paralyzed by the fear that they won't succeed in getting what they want, so they never ever bother to ask for it.

2) They never take the trouble to find out or decide what *exactly* they do want.

3) They're vague in their requests even when they *do* know exactly what they want. Don't be wishy-washy when asking for something, and expect the person you're asking to figure it out. **Know exactly what you want. Be confident. Be specific. Ask for it.**

~~~~~~~~~

Set boundaries for yourself. Know what you can and cannot realistically do. Know what you would or would not want to do. Do not pretend to be okay with a request, or agree to do a favor even if it's the last thing on earth you want to do. Be honest with yourself and with the person making the request. Do not overextend yourself in an effort to please everyone, or with the hope that everyone will like you. Someone has cleverly named that behavior the *Disease to Please*. Do not ever fall prey to that.

Teach others how to treat you. No one has the right to take you for granted, or assume that you'll be okay with anything they dish out. Know from the very start what's okay with you and what's not, and make sure that everyone you interact with knows, as well. First, you must live by your own high standards and values. (Remember the ones you listed in chapter 3). These standards and values will command respect from most people. In cases where they don't, (there are always people who will not observe boundaries without being specifically told), you must, once again, CLEARLY establish your boundaries.

You need to let people know in clear language, and with a confident, serious attitude and tone of voice, that the particular language, behavior, expectation, request - whatever it is - is totally unacceptable to you, if it is. This is another time in your life when you cannot be wishy-washy.

A behavior or request or expectation cannot be okay with you at one time, and not okay the next time. You're young, so it's a tough call, but you must make firm decisions about certain things in your life ahead of time. That way, if or when a difficult situation does arise, you already know your position on the issue, and you're ready to declare it in no uncertain terms.

* * *

Growing Better from the Inside Out!

These are options available to me, but *what do I specifically want?*

become a vet

What is ONE boundary that I will establish for myself?

Stand up for myself

What will I teach others about how to treat me?

tell they they hurt me

* * *

My FIFTH Principle

I Have Beauty That Radiates From the Inside Out

I am the best person I can be, and focus on being truthful, kind, generous, and considerate of others. I use clean language when I speak. I think highly of myself. My inner beauty shows through effortlessly in everything I do, and in my interactions with others.

BEAUTY: grace, magnificence, loveliness, exquisiteness

It really isn't all about your hair, your makeup, or your outfit. Instead, it's really all about your values, your integrity, and your graciousness.

As we go into this chapter on beauty that radiates from the inside out, a story told by Diane Sawyer,

ABC News Anchorwoman, comes to mind. Ms. Sawyer told a story about belonging to a small group of girls called *The Fingernails* when she was a mere schoolgirl. She went on to explain that the girls in this group had chosen the name *The Fingernails* because they considered themselves to be the ones with polish. Got it? Synonyms for *Polish* (in this case) would be similar to the synonyms for *Beauty* above. These girls had a great sense of SELF and confidence! Don't you think?

What are your values?

They are the matters to which you attach the most importance. Do you think that it's important to have the latest fashions and the newest android phone, or do you believe it's important to spend quality time with loved ones and try to help those less fortunate than yourself? Do you think getting a good education is important, or is school just a social environment for you? Do you think it's important to always do your best at the things you endeavor to do? Do you believe that it's important to be trustworthy? Your answers to these questions will tell you what your values are - or what they should be.

What is your integrity?

Do you think it's okay to be insincere about your feelings, fake love, be a hypocritical friend, or break promises? Do you know that if you say you love someone you must mean it, that you must not gossip or lie, and know that if you

> **"Your values, your integrity, and your graciousness are your beauty marks, and your beauty radiates from the inside out."**

make a promise, you must keep it? Do you know that if it becomes impossible to keep your promise, then there must be a good reason why you can't; not just that you don't feel like following through? Do you know that if you're going to break a promise, you need to speak to the person to whom you made the promise and truthfully explain why you can't keep that promise? Do you know that you can't disappoint someone who is depending on your word without good reason? Do you know that you must do the right thing because it is the right thing to do, and not because you think there's a chance you would get caught?

If you only do the right thing when someone is looking, you lack integrity. If you do the right thing simply because it is the right thing to do, you have high integrity; you live according to a high standard of values. Values and integrity are closely intertwined.

What is your graciousness?

Your graciousness is your good, wholesome way of being. You follow *The Golden Rule* and treat others as you would like to be treated. You are kind and considerate. You are honest. You don't speak ill of others. You help where and when you can. You do not use profanity. You are not lewd or vulgar in your way of dress. You are polite to others. You are pleasant. You are generous enough to pay a compliment to a friend instead of thinking of her as your competition, and being hateful. "You're not a hater", to use colloquial tween/teen language.

Your values, your integrity, and your graciousness make up that beauty factor that radiates from the inside out. These traits will be obvious to others when they are in your presence; they will be obvious in your interactions with them. These traits will be the most important aspects of your personality. If you try to live by these high standards all the time, the beauty of the person you truly are will be visible to everyone you encounter, because you will not be faking these qualities. You will not be putting on airs. The behavior that reflects good values, high integrity and graciousness will come to you naturally. You must truly believe in these attributes and try to live by them day by day, hour by hour; in big matters and in small matters.

Avoid being superficial. Statistics show that in the last ten years 66% of girls, by age 15, had had some form of cosmetic surgery; everything from nose jobs to breast implants. You know firsthand that the pressure is on for you to live up to the images of beauty that bombard you coming and going. (72% of girls feel tremendous pressure to be beautiful). Some Girl magazines, like *Seventeen and TeenVogue*, have their own set of criteria for beauty and what makes an IT girl. Your beauty goes deeper than that. You're a *Rockstar Teenage Girl.*

Your values, your integrity, and your graciousness are *your* personal beauty marks.

* * *

Growing Better from the Inside Out!

What are two good values that I have?

_____

_____

Where does my integrity lie?

_____

_____

How can I show my graciousness?

_____

_____

What other quality do I have that I can be proud of?

_____

_____

* * *

My SIXTH Principle

I Do Not Determine My Self-Worth by a Boy's Attention. I Will Also <u>Not</u> Remain in Any Relationship That Becomes Abusive.

I am responsible for my own happiness.
I focus on the things I can do for myself
that build my self-esteem and make me a winner.
I do not subject myself to
abuse in my relationships with boys or with anyone else.

VALUE: worth, merit, usefulness, importance, significance

Sometimes very smart girls are not so smart when it comes to boys. They do well in school, they are leaders in their community, younger girls look up to them, but then when it comes to boys in their own lives, they do silly things. All those smarts go on the back burner.

If a boy ignores you, or does not like you back…does not "crush on you" in return, that's okay. Every boy is not for every girl, and the boy who is for you should be someone quite special. He should be special in his own values and integrity. If he's a "cool" boy and someone who has the attention of many girls, or is chasing after lots of other girls, and thinks he can be careless when it comes to a girl's feelings, he's probably not your best bet anyway.

It's quite nice to be popular. However, it is not always the best thing, if it's only based on trivial things like looks or cool clothes. It's not enough that he's hand-some. It is much better to be sought after because of *who* you are, than because of what you look like.

Don't be hard on yourself because another girl might have caught the attention of a boy you like. You are young. There are other boys who would be more appreciative of you, based on all those beautiful traits mentioned in the previous chapter. You don't, after all, want the attention of someone who really doesn't like you very much. You like him, but he's not interested, let him be. You want someone who really loves you for who you are, and can be a great friend to you; someone who supports your growth and encourages your endeavors.

Build your confidence by focusing on, and excelling in things that you are good at doing. You'll eventually find someone with whom you share common interests, and

"You want someone who really loves you for who you are, and can be a great friend to you; someone who supports your growth and   encourages your endeavors."

that would be far better than having the attention of a popular boy that you have nothing in common with, and who is full of himself and without regard for you or your feelings. **Recognize your own self-worth, as well as the fact that no one can take that away from you.**

Do not engage in an abusive relationship with a young man, or with anyone for that matter.

These days there's a trend in which boys buy girls cell phones in order to keep track of their every move. Teen girls have reported receiving instant messages up to thirty times in an hour. Not only is this wrong, it can be a very dangerous thing for you as a girl. What is a boy showing you when he needs to know where you are, who you're with, and what you're doing every moment of the day? He's showing you that he's possessive, jealous, and insecure. He's also showing that he has a need to control you. It does not mean that he loves you so much that he wants to be in touch with you every minute of the day.

No boy has the right to own (possess) or control you, regardless of how much you think he loves you, or how much *you* think you love *him*. Boys who are

41

controlling and possessive sometimes adopt bad habits like hitting their girlfriends, or verbally abusing them if things don't go their way. He's probably thinking that if your phone isn't answered when he calls, then it must mean that you're with another boy, and that's reason enough for him to mistrust you and abuse you either physically or verbally. Do not fall into that trap!

Don't accept a boy's offers to buy you expensive gifts, or items like cell phones, when he says he just wants to be able to reach you all the time because he loves you so much. The reality is that if he loves you as much as he says he does, he will trust your judgment, allow you to be yourself, give you your personal space, and understand that you have other friends and other interests. He will be happy to grow along with you, rather than try to stifle your growth by making sure you do only the things *he* thinks you should do when he thinks you should do them.

At the first sign of verbal or physical abuse, your instincts must kick in. If he hits you once, he will hit you again. These things begin in a small way at first, maybe a single slap, but do know that over time his violence toward you will escalate. The abuse will become much worse.

As his violence worsens, you will become unsure of yourself; feel diminished in your self-worth. You'll soon be wondering what you did wrong, even

"Abuse changes the way you feel about yourself - and not for the better."

when you know you did nothing wrong. You'll think that you deserve to be hit. You'll soon start thinking that in some way you made him mad, and that this is the punishment you deserve, even if nothing could be further from the truth. Why? Because actions such as these erode your confidence, erode your self-esteem, make you feel less of a person, and make you feel unworthy. Before you know it, you're hiding from him, telling lies so as not to make him angry, sneaking around to meet your friends, getting startled every time the phone rings, engaging in things you really don't want to engage in, all because you are afraid of him. It's a dangerous game to play. Many young girls are in abusive relationships by the time they're fifteen. Sometimes they are so ashamed of themselves, they don't tell their parents or teachers, or other adults about it until they have been seriously hurt, or they end up in a hospital.

Teenagers have done their own research on these problems, and they report a cycle of abuse. On the internet, there are several sites that deal with this topic, including a link from **TEAR** (*Teens Experiencing Abusive Relationships*) that shows the different stages of the abuse cycle, and the roles that the abuser and victim take in each stage. It also depicts the length of time of each stage. An excerpt of the research on the cycle of abuse is featured in this chapter.

With the giant leaps and major improvements in technology (smaller, faster, full-featured phones, video capability, texts, and instant messages) along with cheaper prices and access to more forms of social media, as well as less control of your privacy, the number of cases of violence and abuse among teenagers has greatly increased.

It is very important that you increase your awareness of the problem of abuse in teenage relationships.

KNOW THE CYCLE OF ABUSE

1) The cycle starts with the **GREEN STAGE**, which is exemplified as being a state when both partners are happy to be in a relationship. At this point the relationship is loving and enjoyable.

2) The next stage is the **YELLOW STAGE** in which tension is building within the relationship. The couple might be getting into small arguments, and the abuser might become frustrated with their partner. The victim does their best to reason with the abuser, calm the abuser, and stays away from friends and family to try and work on the relationship. This is the same stage where the abuser is nitpicking at the

victim. The abuser is yelling, screaming, threatening, and blaming everything on the victim. This is also the period where the abuser may act sullen and withdraw affection from the victim. This phase lasts the longest. It could last days, weeks, or months. It could even last for years.

3) The last stage is the **RED STAGE**. This stage is usually the shortest stage and the most harmful. This stage is based on one specific incident that leads to an explosion of anger. The abuser may sexually, physically, psychologically, or verbally harm their partner. Some abusers may use a weapon against the victim, pull their hair, and publicly humiliate the victim. This is the time when the victim may call the police, fight back and/or leave the relationship.

4) The abuser quickly defaults to the **GREEN STAGE** again to make up for his behavior. This is when the abuser will bring flowers, declare his love for the victim, say he is sorry, and may even enter counseling. During this time the abuser will blame outside forces for the abuse, say he is stressed, and make empty promises that things will change. The victim at this time will fail to alert parents, end all legal procedures, if any, against the abuser, go back to the relationship, agree to work things out, and feel hopeful that things will change.

When things become comfortable again, the abuse can start all over again. Once the cycle is in place it becomes difficult to break. The cycle of abuse is based around **denial**, because when the both parties deny the abuse, there is no way to stop the pattern.

It is very important to know and recognize the cycle of abuse if it occurs. The information can save you or your friends from mental or physical violence and abuse. Spot the tendency early and get out of the relationship quickly. Enlist the help of a trusted adult, if it becomes necessary to do so.

* * *

Growing Better from the Inside Out!

When it comes to romantic relationships, what will I do?

_____

_____

_____

When it comes to abusive relationships, what will I NOT do?

_____

_____

_____

What other promises can I make to myself?

_____

_____

_____

What should I know about the cycle of abuse? How can I avoid it?

_____

_____

_____

* * *

My SEVENTH Principle

I Do Not Allow Myself to Be a Victim of Cyberbullying. I Also Stay Away from Adult Websites, and Keep Myself Safe from Strangers I Encounter on Social Networks.

I terminate friendships that draw me into gossip, meanness, and spreading rumors on social networks, as well as friendships that cause me to have negative feelings about myself. By keeping myself safe, and by respecting others, I show that I care about myself and respect myself.

VICTIM: injured party, sufferer, wounded, duped, prey

In today's world, social networks are a major part of life. There is almost nothing you can do without being a part of them, or being exposed to them in some way, shape, or form. You might not be actively participating in the daily back and forth conversations or profile updates on *FaceBook*, or following anyone on *Twitter.* You might not have space on *My Space*, and you might not be *"Linked In"*. However, you might be surprised that your name is somewhere out there in cyberspace. Chances are that you can type your name into the Google box, and see information come up about yourself and your accomplishments or current status that you didn't post. There might even be pictures of you that you didn't put out there yourself, and didn't know existed. Your name might be included or attached to someone else's name. The information might be simple; you're still very young. Maybe you'll only show up there as the relative of someone who is on the site for a bigger reason, like having won a prestigious award or invented a game.

It's an amazing thing! It doesn't matter why you're in these public forums; the fact is you're there. You're out there, exposed to the world.

If you voluntarily participate in these social networks, you need to consider what image of yourself you want to present to the public. You *do* need to be self-respecting, and respectful to others. You also need to be very careful about your personal safety. Why all of these conditions for participating in social networks? There are a million reasons. Let's list some of them:

You don't want anyone to get the wrong impression of you, so don't post naked pictures of yourself on the internet. Also, don't use foul language. Don't engage in suggestive or sexual conversations with others. Doing so will make you appear loose and vulgar, and as someone who does not have any respect for herself.

Less than 10 years ago, 71% of teens considered boyfriends/girlfriends spreading rumors about them via cell phones and social networking sites a serious problem. You can be sure that this number has increased with the arrival of more modern technology.

You shouldn't tolerate being gossiped about, or trashed, or threatened, or bullied on these networks. If such a situation arises, immediately bring it to the attention of your parents, teachers, or other trusted adult and *discontinue your membership or participation on the site immediately.* The temptation is to stay on and write posts in your own defense, return the criticism, or just see who else is saying what about you. Don't Do It! Get off the site. Alert an adult.

> **"The girl bullying phenomenon involves gossip, mind games, violence, victimization, harassment, and plain old meanness."**

Very important: Do not let negative things that others say or post about you give you negative feelings about who you truly are, or cause you to doubt yourself and your own potential for success and happiness. That's one of the reasons it's important to discontinue your participation immediately. You don't want the negative notions of others entering your mind, and keeping you from experiencing your own joy and bliss.

You need to avoid getting drawn into gossiping, trashing schoolmates, creating false rumors, making threats, or engaging in any other form of bullying. Don't be the bully. It's the old Golden Rule that says "Do unto others as you would have them do unto you." In other words, if you wouldn't like it for yourself, don't do it to someone else. Don't even share information that you know to be true about others. Their affairs or issues are not yours to discuss. By respecting others, you show that you respect yourself. Someone who is respectful to others and self-respecting is a lot less likely to be a victim of disrespect. It can still happen. There are people who will be meanspirited to others no matter what. However, it is more unlikely that it will happen to you if it's something you stay away from in the first place. It's that other old cliché that says "You reap what you sow", or "you get what you give."

You're not an adult, so adult websites are not for you. Block pop-ups on your computer so that you are not accidentally exposed to adult websites, and tempted to click on them out of curiosity. Once you click on the site, the host assumes you're interested and will keep up the campaign to draw you in. The pop-up is a gateway. Do not open it.

Stay Safe!

- **Don't interact with strangers on the internet**, or with people who befriend you for the wrong reason. Never post details of your address or whereabouts, or give out any other personal information. Don't advertise that your parents will be, or are presently away on vacation and that you're in charge of your younger siblings, or home alone. Don't accept invitations to chat rooms when you don't know the participants. That's a sure way to bring dangerous persons, even criminals, into your life. Always focus on staying safe.

- **Don't agree to physically meet a stranger; not even in a public place.** Meeting in a public place gives you a false sense of security. The reality is that all the other people around cannot protect you. They'll automatically assume that you know the person you're with. Most dangerous types will not approach you with a hostile look, or with an exposed weapon that would cause others to come to your rescue. Instead, they'll approach you with a smile and keep smiling as they threaten to do something harmful to you, if you don't willingly follow their orders. They're confidence artists. They present a false image of themselves so you let your guard down. All the Amber Alerts and photos of your face on milk cartons won't help you after something bad happens.

This is not meant to scare you. It is meant to make you think about these possibilities before you're in a position where you're being forced to make a quick decision. Ill-intentioned types will usually try to get you to decide quickly; not give you time to think things through and see the danger in their plans. It's a simple warning that bears repeating:

> *NEVER arrange to meet a stranger <u>anywhere</u> for <u>any</u> <u>reason</u>—not for a modeling contract; not for a chance to go to Hollywood. Never go off to physically meet a stranger. NEVER, EVER!*

Growing Better from the Inside Out!

How will I limit my participation and interactions on social networks?

_____

_____

_____

If I become the victim of cyberbullying, or if I feel vulnerable in any way, what will I do?

I cut or try to commit

suiduice

_____

If I know that a friend is being bullied or threatened, who will I alert?

My parent or

adult

_____

* * *

Ode to a Teenage Girl

And so I will create
A poem for her
Something that befits both her beauty
And her sense of self;
For oft when we were meshed in conversation—
When we matched thought with thought
I certainly did see
Something of my yesteryear—
My teenage years--
Indeed a somewhat sisterness,
But more—an almost twinship
Born from baring souls,
Catching tears that didn't quite fall
And sharing laughter—
Laughter soft as breaking glass
And it is as the poet John Keats said:
"A thing of beauty is a joy forever."
The same is true of beauteous teenage souls--
They, too, most surely are
An everlasting joy.

RockStar Teenage Girl

SELF and Confidence Building for Tween & Teenage Girls

Book 2
7 Spiritual Principles

My FIRST Principle

I Am, First and Foremost, a Divine Being.

*I am God's own special creation; I am exactly the way
I was meant to be. I accept myself for who I am.*

DIVINE: godly, heavenly, celestial, blissful

**Each and every human being was made by the same power
and the same force that made everything else in the universe.** You may call that force God, or you may use
another name. However, it is the creative force, and it
is divine and good. Everything it creates, therefore, is
also inherently divine and good.

Think of the sky and the ocean, the mountains, the
trees, the birds, the fish, and the animals of the jungle. All were made by that creative and divine force.

When something is divine, there is nothing imperfect about it. Do you ever think that one bird is better than the other, or that one elephant is superior to another? You don't. Do you think that a giraffe is better than a lion? No. They are simply *different* from one another. So, too, are you simply different from other human beings. You're not superior or inferior. You are just different.

The force that created you determined that you were worthy of life, and created you in exactly your form; endowed with the special traits you have. You were not intended to be a cat or a daffodil. You were not meant to be a tree, or for that matter, another girl. You were made exactly the way God wanted you to be. That's pretty special when you think about it. Say it out loud to yourself: "*God wanted me to be exactly who I am.*" Repeat that statement to yourself several times until you fully grasp the reality, the truth, and the importance of it.

Just think: God wanted *you*, and created *you* exactly the way you are out of his wonderful, creative power. It is the same for every other girl; she was made exactly

> **"God wanted you, and created you exactly the way you are, out of his wonderful, creative power".**

the way that she was meant to be. You can look at the physical and personality differences between you and your friends and know with all certainty that each of you is exactly the way you were meant to be; each of you being a different expression of God.

If birds and elephants are different in their size and features, but are equally special in their own way, then how much *more so* are you who have a soul? Everything that is alive in the universe came out of God's imagination, as did you. No one, therefore, is better than you. The creative force did not choose to bring them to life, and leave you out. Just as a bird was not meant to be an elephant or a different kind of bird, so you, too, were not meant to be someone else.

Therefore, be content to be exactly who you are, and give expression to the divine aspect of yourself every day. No other living creature or person is exactly like you. Since you came from a divine source, you are also divine. Just as apples are like their parent trees and roses are of the same nature as the rose bushes they come from, so too are you part of the divinity that created you. Divinity is your essence, your makeup, your being. You are exactly like the divine source from which you came. Be happy, then, about your looks, your level of intelligence, and all the other qualities you have, like your sense of humor, your generosity, your sensitivity, your kindness to others.

You are divine because you came from a divine source.

Growing Better from the Inside Out!

What evidence do I see in myself that tells me I'm a divine being?

_____

_____

_____

_____

_____

How can I nurture the divine aspect of myself?

_____

_____

_____

_____

_____

My SECOND Principle

I Am God's Unique Creation, with Special Gifts and Talents That Are All My Own.

Within me are special gifts and talents. I can use these gifts and talents to create or achieve anything my heart desires, and to become anyone I want to be.

TALENT: gift, flair, aptitude, capacity, genius

Whatever you desire to do, you are able to do. This is such a simple statement that it probably seems almost silly to you, or you're probably thinking that you've heard it a thousand times. The fact is, though, that it is a plain and simple truth, and nothing but the truth. The mere fact that you have the *desire* to do or achieve a particular thing, or to reach a particular goal, means that you already have within you the potential and the tools that are necessary to achieve it, become it, or do it.

Think about it! There are certain things that you just would never ever consider taking on; they just never cross your mind at all as something you could do or would want to do. For me, it's flying an airplane. I have never ever considered doing that; not as a job, not as a hobby. I will always buy a plane ticket and have someone else fly me to where I want to go. I have, however, always written, and always think of writing; poems, stories, reports, compositions, books, letters, everything - anything.

When I need to send a Thank You or Birthday card to a friend or relative, I buy cards that are blank on the inside, just so I could write in them. Friends tell me they enjoy reading the e-mail they get from me. Go figure! Email! I do believe that writing is one of the things that I was born to do, and hopefully would do in such a way that it would be useful and beneficial to others; like writing this book for you.

When we are born and arrive in the world as babies, we bring with us special gifts and talents, and we also arrive with all of the qualities and abilities needed to achieve the

> **"Whatever it is that you love doing most, or long to do, is the area in which your God-given talent usually lies."**

goals we will set for ourselves later in life. Of course,

we don't know it at the time, and unfortunately, some people never get to find out, but we are *all* born with the seeds of all our capabilities already in us. Some are born with the ability to be fashion designers, others are born to be artists or writers, some were born with the ability to be heart surgeons, yet others to be great at sports, or the performing arts.

Whatever it is that you *love* doing most is the area in which your special talent usually lies. Of course, you might be good at several things, or love doing several things, which just means that you have several special seeds of capability.

To find out what *your* special gifts and talents are, ask yourself these questions: What am I most happy doing? In what activity am I involved when I lose track of time? What am I going to do today that makes me excited about getting out of bed? What could I do as a job that I would still do even if I didn't get paid to do it? The answers to these questions will give you a clue about your calling, your special gifts, your dharma (your purpose - the thing or things that you were born to do).

Also, if you notice that there are certain things you do which always get comments and compliments, then that might be your area of strength. Do you have an eye for color and design and always put together beautiful outfits for yourself that catch the attention of others? Are people amazed by your voice when they hear you sing? Do you get the lead role in the school play and perform it exceptionally well? Are you the one who brings stray or wounded animals home and nurse them back to health, or do you love teaching or working with younger children? Does your debate team win debates because of the strength and delivery of the points you make? Are you able to easily influence others?

If you answered yes to any of these questions, or to other questions that you might have posed to yourself, these answers are all clues about the abilities that you have. It will be up to you to nurture your special talents, create more opportunities for yourself to use them, and develop them to their full potential, so that *you* can reach your fullest potential.

> **The Good News:** *Your very own special gifts and talents are with you all the time.*

Growing Better from the Inside Out!

What is one special gift or talent I have that I can develop?

_____

_____

_____

_____

_____

How does my gift or talent show my uniqueness?

_____

_____

_____

_____

_____

When or where can I possibly use my gift or talent for the benefit of others?

_____

_____

_____

* * *

My THIRD Principle

I Can Trust My Own Nature to Help Me Make the Best Decisions and Lead Me Down the Right Path.

I came into the world with divine wisdom.
All I have to do is listen
closely to my heart, remember that
I am part of a source that is
all-knowing, and trust the guidance
I receive from within.

TRUST: depend on, expect, rely on, believe in

It is important, as a tween or teenage girl who is on her way to womanhood, to listen closely to your heart. Listen to yourself. Examine your own thoughts about your life, and see the path you're taking. This path is outside of your school life. On the path of your school life, you'll be pursuing a course of study, and there are certain things that you'll just have to do if you're going to be a successful student.

The path to which we are referring, is the path of your personal life. What decisions do you need to make about friendships with other girls, or friendships and romantic relationships with boys? How will you care for your soul? How will you protect your self-image and self-esteem from becoming eroded? How will you build your self-confidence? How will you be true to yourself and the divinity with which you were born? How can you be your best self? These are all questions that need to be answered at this very important stage of your life.

If you sit quietly with yourself and truly desire to answer these questions in a positive way, you will know where you are, and where to go with your life. *It might take time.* Don't expect that you will pose these questions to yourself one morning and in fifteen minutes have a clear answer set in stone. You can also expect changes in your path as you grow older, have new experiences, and need to make different decisions. This soul-searching is an ongoing process. At several junctures in your life, you'll be listening closely to that heart of yours and hearing what it is saying to you about each question.

For one thing, it will always let you know that you *can* do whatever it is you *really* want to do. However, there will be people in your life who will tell you that you cannot, or should not be doing that wonderful something that your heart is set on. The doubt and naysaying might come from your own mind; not from your heart, but from your mind. Try to discern the difference between the two sources.

Listen to yourself. Trust your own nature. That is not to say that you should never seek the advice of a parent, a friend, or a trusted adult, but ten chances to one, your heart will lead you in the right direction if you're honest with yourself. Weigh your options. See how each one feels in your gut when you choose it. The one that gives you a good feeling, makes you feel calm, makes you feel relaxed and peaceful when you choose it, is the one that's right for you. Be prepared to be clear, but patient and respectful with a parent or other adult who might be totally bent on having you make a different decision. For example, your mom and dad want you to start gearing up to attend medical school; you want to become a cosmetologist. Since fourth grade you've been doing the hair and nails of your girlfriends and you're great at it. Doing it also makes you happy. It's the thing you would do even if you didn't get paid for it. **Follow your passion.**

Now it's time to choose a high school, and you're not applying to a high school for science which would lead you to medical school. You're filling out forms for the vocational schools. You're also looking into a high school for the performing arts because in addition to your knack for doing hair and nails, you've been told that your singing voice is "crazy good". Maybe it's time for college and you want to go into a pre-law program. You want to become a lawyer who will advocate for the underprivileged. You really have no interest in accounting. You don't want to become a CPA like your father. You could have a major fight on your hands. Trust your gut. If you must go along with the wishes of your parents for now (after all, they're probably paying your tuition), keep the fire alive in your heart for the things that make you truly happy.

Try discussing your position and feelings on the matter when things are calm and your parents are more open to hearing what you have to say. You might be able to change majors after the first term. In the meantime, keep honing your skills in those special areas you like, and in the things you're good at. Take that dance class as an elective. Work in a beauty salon on weekends and watch the pros at work. The time will come when choices and decisions are totally yours to make, and you'll have no trouble knowing what to do.

There was recently a news story about a lawyer who went all the way through law school, passed the Bar with flying colors, and began his career as a lawyer. Soon, he became a partner in a law firm. After years of working successfully in that profession, he realized that his heart was unfulfilled. He wanted to make cakes. He quit working as a lawyer to become a baker of the finest cakes in Brooklyn, New York. It was always what his heart had told him he should do. He had baked cakes alongside his mother as a young boy and had developed a love for baking. Because his heart was in the cake-making business, he became very good at it, and very successful with it. The cake-making business has now become a very lucrative source of income for him, and he couldn't be any happier waking up every morning to begin working at something he truly loves.

Elizabeth Gilbert, Author of *Eat, Pray, Love*, said the following to an audience one day during an interview with Oprah Winfrey: "Ask yourself, what do I really, really, really want?" (Gilbert says that you must say the word *really* three times) Well, maybe, maybe not, but the point is this: **you must ask that question of yourself, listen closely for the answer from within, and then follow your heart.**

* * *

Growing Better from the Inside Out!

How can I tell which decision is coming from my mind, and which is coming from my heart?

_____

_____

_____

_____

_____

_____

_____

_____

Follow your heart. By doing so, you are putting yourself on the path to your greatest happiness.

* * *

My FOURTH Principle

I Receive the Right Opportunities from the Universe When I Am Ready To Learn or Accomplish Something.

*I need never be anxious or distressed about
any situation. I can enjoy my life and
be relaxed, knowing that everything
will turn out well for me.*

OPPORTUNITY: occasion, chance, break, prospect, opening

The universe is benevolent and kind; it wants to help you create your highest good. This is a big concept for a tween or teenager to fully grasp. You might simply have to accept that concept without quite understanding it for now. As you grow older, as you spend time thinking about this, or as evidence of this truth becomes part of your experience, you'll fully grasp the meaning of it, and more important, come to believe it. Maybe a parent or other adult you know has already seen the proof of this. Now, *there's* a conversation you can have with an adult in your life.

It is a good idea to draw from the wisdom and experience of others. There's also this chance—the chance that you are having that very experience now. Maybe the fact that you are reading this book is an example of the universe sending you the right people, the right tool, or the right opportunity because you are ready to learn or accomplish something.

Think about it. You might be about to leave the nurturing and protective walls of your middle school; a school where teachers still call your parents about missed assignments or grades that could be better. You might be going through your high school years, preparing to move on to college. The group of friends you love and trust, and who came through middle and high school with you would be soon disbanding.

In college, you'll have to be much more autonomous; there'll be big decisions you must make on your own. Parents might not be around to guide your every step. Familiar faces and voices might be far away. You must now depend on yourself and your own good judgment a whole lot more. You need to know that the universe is cooperative and nurturing, and that you have only to trust that you'll be given the help and the guidance you need when you need it. Know that there are no coincidences. Seemingly haphazard events are all part of the universe's orchestration of experiences that lead you to a successful life, whether or not you recognize them as such at the time that they are happening to you. **Expect kindness. Expect assistance from the right people at the right time.**

Not so long ago, a woman, Shelley, was sharing with a women's group she belonged to, that she had come up with an invention and was wondering how to protect it. She didn't think she could afford a patent attorney. As it happened, the new neighbor, let's call her Sally, who had just moved in next door and who just happened to be having a casual conversation with her, mentioned that she *was* a patent attorney, tired of the city and wanting to live in a friendly, more close-knit community. As the two women exchanged information about themselves, Sally told Shelley that she would gladly help her with the process and paperwork necessary for getting a patent for her invention. She also said she would do this totally free of charge.

In exchange, Shelley, who was a seamstress and who had dabbled in interior decorating on a small scale, volunteered to make Sally all the drapes that she needed for her new home, and share some decorating tips, also free of charge. Was this meeting or conversation mere coincidence? Was it orchestration by the universe of events in both these women's lives that brought each of them a good and favorable outcome? What do you think? Has something like that ever happened to you? Think back to a time when you got just what you needed when you needed it, and without much or any effort on your part.

Someone you know might have had an experience just like Shelley's. He or she might have thought that it was mere coincidence – or maybe it was seen as the universe's way of assisting them. Some spiritual leaders say that there are no coincidences in life; that everything happens for a reason. Some also believe that everything in the universe is exactly the way it was meant to be, and that there are lessons to be learned on a daily basis, if we would only pay attention.

Neal Donald Walsh in his book *Conversations with God* tells us that the universe helps us every step of the way; that the answer to a burning question that you have could be in the lyrics of the next song you happen to hear on the radio. The answer might already be in your heart, and the song serves as confirmation. Someone could hand you just the business card you need, or a total stranger will give you advice when you're stuck between your head and your heart not knowing what to do. It's just that simple. The answer to your question or dilemma is not going to be given to you by a booming voice from the sky. It will probably be given to you by the voice of a stranger or new friend, or a close relative. It might even sound like your own voice talking to yourself, but when you hear it, you'll recognize it as the voice of your heart; the voice of your divine self. Pay attention to it.

Ask questions of your heart. It will always guide you in the right direction. If you think you have two options, pose them both to yourself. One of them will feel comfortable in the pit of your stomach, and one will not… and you will feel this physically. The one that feels comfortable and gives you a feeling of relief and ease about the particular situation or dilemma is the one that you should pursue. The advice you should pursue comes from the voice of a higher power. It might come, as we said, as your own voice or your own thoughts. How would you know that it's your divine, spiritual guidance, and not just the babbling of your mind?

In his book, *Conversations with God*, Neal Donald Walsh quotes God as saying:

"Mine is always the Highest Thought, your Clearest Word, your Grandest Feeling. Anything less is from another source. The Highest Thought is always that thought which contains joy. The Clearest Words are those words which contain truth. The Grandest Feeling is that feeling which you call love. Joy. Truth. Love. These three are interchangeable, and one always leads to the other. It matters not in which order they are placed."

Take some time to examine the feelings that are associated with your decision. Does your decision *feel* right? That is your truth. Do you *feel* that you are being lead to the accomplishment of your purpose without hurting yourself or anyone else? If so, your feelings are coming from a place of love. Do you *feel* a sense of ease and peace about your decision? This is your joy. Look for these feelings around your decisions. Identify them one at a time.

Trust your heart. Trust your gut. Your divine soul which is part of the soul of God, speaks to you through your deepest feelings.

* * *

Growing Better from the Inside Out!

Can I think of a time when everything just worked out for me, or when everything just fell into place without my having to try too hard?

_____

_____

_____

_____

_____

This is my story:

_____

_____

_____

_____

_____

* * *

My FIFTH Principle

I Attract Great Experiences into My Life by Having Only Positive Thoughts About Myself and My Goals, and the Knowledge That Everything I Am, or Think, I Will Attract Into My Life.

*I know that I can attract into my life
anything that I want. I know what I want
to achieve, and I leave no room for
doubt about my capabilities. I am part of
the same powerful source that creates all things.*

**POSITIVE: optimistic, constructive,
upbeat, encouraging, assured**

You are part of that source which has the power and potential to create all things. Therefore, you should have no doubt that everything you desire, you can have: good health, success, riches, great relationships, and happiness. The source from which you were born knows no lack, and knows no imperfection. There is nothing it cannot do, or cannot create. The universe is a source of ultimate intelligence. Its intelligence lies in its ability to manifest in the life of each person whatever he or she really wants. The intelligence of the universe is not the same as academic knowledge. Instead, the intelligence of the universe is the orchestration of timing and opportunity and people you need in your life, to bring about the things that you imagine for yourself; *and it does begin with your imagination*.

It is therefore very important, actually it is crucial, to imagine your life as you want it to be, and develop the feeling in yourself that you would have when you do indeed see your desires come to life. Experience that feeling now. Once your imagination gets you to the place that you want to be, **feel** that you're already there, already have it, or already have accomplished it. That's exhilarating, isn't it?

You should take this one step further and get to this place in your imagination and this feeling of already having reached your goal, just before you fall asleep. Do you feel

> **"The feeling that you already have what you want, or are who you aspire to be, is paramount to the success and the actual accomplishment of your goal."**

powerful, happy, content, successful, rich? (*Don't forget that being rich encompasses more than financial wealth. It also includes your health, your relationships, your optimistic outlook, your sense of wholeness and well-being*). Are you enjoying your achievements, or whatever it is that you imagine for yourself? Clear your mind of the day's other activities or thoughts, go to the visualization and feeling of your success and drift off into sleep. The power of your subconscious, which will be very much at work while you're asleep, is the generating power behind all of your goals and dreams.

Your imagination, feelings, and subconscious mind work together to make your dreams a reality. Try it. See for yourself. Start with something small and work from there if that's a big concept for you right now, and you're a little cynical about the truth of it.

Do you engage in self-talk that is negative? Negative self-talk says that you can't really make your dreams and goals a reality. Here are some examples of negative self-talk:

- I Can't
- I'm too young
- No one will help me
- I'm probably not good enough

- I need to be smarter (*prettier, taller, cooler, richer, part of the popular clique*)
- No one has ever done this before, what makes me think I can…

When negative self-talk begins to form in your mind, or when you become aware that it has already been your thinking, **knock it off! Stop it right there**. *Consciously take on a positive thought.* Here are some examples of positive self-talk:

- I can do this
- I'm perfectly suited for accomplishing this
- The right opportunities and people will come into my life to help me
- I'm worthy; absolutely good enough
- I already am all the things I need to be, and already have the potential to accomplish my dreams and goals
- I can be the first to do this

Everything you see in the world is an expression of the intelligence of the universe. Think about the ocean, the rain forest, the mountains, sand on the beach; all created out of universal intelligence.

Think about people you know who are successful: Nobel Peace Prize winners, presidents, best-selling authors, famous singers, artists, musicians. All of these people imagined something for themselves, believed in it, felt excited about it, thought about it all the time, knew they already had the power to achieve it in them, and kept that dream alive until it became their reality.

Here are a few simple steps to succeeding in all of your endeavors:

You must know who you are: a field of pure potential, of perfection, of power, of possibility - all possibility. That is the source from which you were born.

1) **Imagine what you want to accomplish or who you strive to be**—clearly and very specifically. There is power in the words "I Am." Say out loud, "I Am_____."

2) **Generate a feeling of fulfillment, happiness, and gratitude** for having achieved your goal or wish (even if you're not yet there).

3) **Let your goal or wish be your mind's focus**, both when you're awake and are actively working on achieving your dream and just before you fall asleep, so that your subconscious mind can orchestrate the details of your accomplishment while you sleep.

This is one of the most important lessons that you can learn:

"What you believe and feel about yourself and your accomplishments deep down in your subconscious, you will achieve or manifest in your real or waking life.

It is your subconscious mind that rules and determines what your life actually becomes."

Growing Better from the Inside Out!

What do I really believe, deep down in my heart, about myself and the things that I want to achieve ?

_____

_____

_____

_____

_____

_____

_____

_____

_____

_____

_____

_____

MY REALLY BIG DREAMS

_____

_____

_____

_____

_____

_____

_____

_____

_____

_____

_____

_____

_____

* * *

My SIXTH Principle

I Find Happiness Within Myself. It is My Birthright. I Do Not Seek It from an External Source. It Is Part of My Spiritual Makeup.

Happiness is part of my spiritual makeup. It is already in me and available to me the minute that I choose it. Being happy is what I choose.

BIRTHRIGHT: legacy, inheritance, gift, bequest, heritage

Don't make the mistakes that some grownups make. Many Grownups get so caught up with **seeking** happiness or **waiting** to be happy, that they forget to enjoy life. They think - and believe - that more money, a bigger house, more of whatever they think they like now, will make them happy when they have more of it. Some grownups **wait** to be happy. They say, "When I get a bigger home, I will start inviting my friends over and enjoy spending quality time with them," or "when I retire I will enjoy my hobbies, and then my life will be happier."

In the meantime they keep doing the things they'd rather not do, like *not* spending time enjoying the friendships they've already established, and *not* taking time out to engage in a hobby that brings them joy. They think they'll do the cake-making or the knitting or the art, or the ballroom dancing when they retire, because then they'll have time. All the while, life is slipping by, and their happiness becomes just a dream about the future.

> **"Happiness depends upon ourselves."**
> *Aristotle*

Our happiness is dependent on the choices we make, and we know that choice is a very powerful thing. We therefore need to *choose to be happy.*

One way that you can choose happiness is to decide to appreciate and be grateful for all the loved ones in your life, and all the good experiences you have on a daily basis. Be grateful for a hug from a parent, the smile of your sister or brother when you enter the room (it means they're happy to see you). Even a compliment from your teacher on an assignment you've completed could add to your happiness today.

If something is not going so well in your opinion, then make a conscious decision to let it go. Do not hold a grudge. Do not keep thinking of the negative thing someone might have said about you; playing it over and over in your mind. Know that whatever that person's judgment was, is not who you truly are. Dig deep into your well of self-confidence and move on from that negativity.

There's one more important thing: Do not spend precious time planning how to "get someone back" for what they did to you or said about you. If it's a close friend, and your feelings have been hurt, you can choose to address the matter with him or her in a calm manner and with kindness. Do not be accusatory. Say instead, "I value our friendship, and my feelings were hurt by your words or your actions…"

Don't walk up to this person or these persons with an enraged attitude, calling him, her, or them unkind names, and threatening to get even. You might not be immediately able to discuss the matter calmly. In that case, your best bet would be to separate yourself both physically and mentally from the situation.

Wait until you think you can handle the matter kindly and intelligently. Maybe after some time has passed, you might think that the particular wrongdoing wasn't that important or that horrible after all, and decide to just let the whole thing go.

Dr. Phil McGraw who is a psychologist, and known as an expert on relationships and solving problematic situations, always asks the guests on his show: "Do you want to be happy, or do you want to be right?" It's kind of funny when he asks it, but usually you can see the guest stop and think for about two seconds, and then choose to be happy. Once the guest has *made the choice* to be happy, he or she becomes receptive to the expert's advice and suggestions for mending the relationship, or solving the problem. The rest is easy.

Once you make the decision to be happy, you'll immediately, or almost immediately, experience a sense of calm and of peace, and feel the happiness which is already in you.

Being happy is a choice.
Choose to be happy today.

* * *

Growing Better from the Inside Out!

Today I choose to be happy about this life situation:

_____

_____

_____

_____

_____

_____

_____

_____

_____

_____

_____

_____

Today I choose to change this life situation, or stop being unhappy about it:

_____

_____

_____

_____

_____

_____

_____

_____

_____

_____

_____

_____

* * *

My SEVENTH Principle

I Tap Into Divine Consciousness, of Which I Am Already a Part, in Order to Access My Power, My Peace, My Potential, and My Bliss.

When I align myself with my true and divine nature which is all power, all possibility, all joy, all happiness, I am able to manifest in my life, everything that I desire to do, have, and be.

Potential: capability, aptitude, ability, possibility

Although we are awake, we are unconscious most of the time. We are unconscious because we are trapped in our thoughts: our thoughts about ourselves, our friends, past situations, future possibilities. How can we be unconscious if we are having thoughts might be your next thought in the form of a question. The answer is this: *our mind with all its thoughts about ourselves is not who or what we truly are.* Who and what we truly are is the consciousness that allows us to perceive with our senses and interpret with our minds. This

> "Our mind with all its thoughts, is not who or what we truly are".

consciousness is divine. This consciousness is all powerful. This consciousness gave rise in physical form to everything that is in the universe. This consciousness has infinite creative power. We must step away from the thoughts and judgments of our minds in order to tap into that pure and divine consciousness; to become awake. This is a very difficult concept to grasp. Indeed, it is a very difficult concept to explain.

Eckhart Tolle, in his best-selling books *The Power of Now* and *A New Earth* explains that consciousness exists only in the present time, and says that we must **be in the NOW** in order to experience consciousness fully. The present moment is the only thing that's real. Thoughts of the past are not real because they are not present. Once the moment has passed, it is simply a memory. Thoughts of the future are not real either. They're an imagination or anticipation. Only the present moment is real, and being in the present moment, being in the Now, is the only time that we're fully conscious, or can experience consciousness as being our true essence; or true nature. That consciousness is who we truly are.

In order to experience ourselves we must quiet the chatter in our minds. We must cease our judgment of things or situations as being good or bad. Tolle goes on to say that things just are the way they are at the time, and that it is our thought and perception of these situations that can bring us joy or misery. Once we begin to wish that the situation that exists were otherwise, we begin to fight against it in our minds and begin to be unhappy. If we accept what is, in the moment that it is, we are aligned with the present, and therefore aligned with consciousness. Rather than attempting to explain further, let's outline one simple way that the author suggests for putting the mind on *pause* in order to access divine consciousness. **Being conscious allows us to access our power, our peace, our potential, and our bliss.**

Many pathways to accessing power, peace, potential and bliss have been suggested through the ages. Meditation is one pathway that millions of people use. In fact, there is a place in the United States called Fairfield, Iowa, where the residents meditate twice every day. It is said to be the happiest place in America. Adults do it; children do it, too. In one of their Kindergarten to 12th grade schools, meditation is part of the daily routine. For the younger children aged four to ten who might have a little trouble being still for an extended period of time, there is a walking meditation. The students walk around as they meditate on a single word that they've been given. This particular form of meditation practiced in Fairfield by its residents (and there are many forms of this practice) is called Transcendental Meditation, and it is practiced by people all over the world. Its origin is India.

We will, however, examine the simplest of meditative practices. It's the simplest because it is available to all of us, all of the time. We're talking about focusing on the breath. We breathe involuntarily. We do not think about breathing (that's barring a visit to the doctor's office when he asks us to take a deep breath, and then breathe out. That's really the only time we think about our breathing). Breathing is just one of those intelligent things that the body does without help from the mind. Same goes for the heartbeat, digestion, and the circulation of blood through the system. These processes go on for all the years that we're alive, never needing any help from our minds. How amazing is it that we never have to think that the heart should now be sending blood to the veins and that we need to send it a reminder.

That's pretty cool, isn't it?

Let's go back to the process for accessing consciousness. The process for tapping into consciousness, into the present, into the **Now,** requires simple observation of the breath. At first, this might not be easily possible without some background thoughts in the mind.

The mind is in the habit of always presenting thoughts to us; thoughts that it wants us to believe are important. The truth is that these thoughts are not important. They're either past or future, or our own opinion and judgment of things. (For example, that's not a nice dress that lady is wearing. That boy hurt my feelings yesterday. If my cousin Carol calls tomorrow, I will tell her… I hate having to do homework. I probably won't do well on the debate team. I'll probably get only a C on the test. I'm sure you get the picture).

However, the process of quieting the mind and aligning with the present, becoming conscious, becomes easier with practice. The exercise does not have to be lengthy either. Short periods of being aware of our breath each day will be enough to connect us to the present; to consciousness. It is said to be more beneficial to do this several times during the course of a day, than to do hours of meditation, as we know it, once or twice a week. Notice that it is not possible to think about the past or the future, or to make judgments about situations while observing the breath. The breath becomes the only focus. Notice, if you will, the feeling of peace and calm that arises as a result of quieting the thoughts of the mind. In the process of observing the breath, past and future events are of no concern. We are fully present - and conscious - fully engaged with, and fully in, the present moment. We have only awareness, which is our essence; who we truly are.

Frequent practice of this process is one way that you can access your power and peace and potential and bliss. The great thing about that is the fact that you can choose this way of being conscious and experiencing your true self as often as you like, at any time, in any place, and under any circumstance.

You can always focus on your breath in order to experience consciousness; yourself.

* * *

Growing Better from the Inside Out!

How many times during the course of a day would I focus on my breath, in order to align myself with my pure state; consciousness; the essence of who I am?

_____

_____

_____

_____

_____

_____

_____

_____

_____

* * *

RockStar Teenage Girl

SELF and Confidence Building for Tween & Teenage Girls

Bonus:
The Eighth Principle

My EIGHTH Principle

In Whatever Way That I Can, And Whenever Possible, I Strive to Be of Service to Others. Being of Service is My Highest Purpose of All.

In my daily living, I will strive to be of service to others. As one link of the human chain, I know that all human beings are part of the divine whole, as am I. Because we are all connected, I serve myself in serving others. Serving others takes nothing away from me. Instead, it adds to the connectedness of humanity.

SERVICE: help, assistance, use, benefit, advantage

This eighth principle is a bonus principle. It can fall under the category of either your personal principles or your spiritual principles. Being of service can be part of your graciousness and beauty that radiate from the inside out, or it can be the highest of your spiritual principles. You might agree that this principle straddles both categories, and can at one and the same time be both personal and spiritual.

Being of service might seem like a big concept, or a lot to expect from a tween or teenage girl. The idea sounds like it should be something expected of adults. However, it's actually very simple. The question is simply: How can I serve, or be of help to another human being? At this time, that other human being might be a family member, a friend, someone at school who needs a friend, or an organization in your community.

You can probably be a mentor to a younger girl at a Boys and Girls Club one day a week, or to a neighbor's child who has no siblings. Basically, being of service is just a grander way of thinking about volunteering or helping. When you volunteer to do something, you do it without being asked, you do it willingly, you do it because you see a need, and you do it because you want to help someone else. These reasons for volunteering are also the key concepts behind being of service, and you are not too young to start being of service to others.

At the end of it all, being of service to others is the very highest purpose of your life.

* * *

You Are Divine Consciousness

You are Divine Consciousness
You were born of That.
In a moment of total and divine power
You came to be.
It were as though God breathed
A breath so strong, so mighty,
So perfect, so complete,
So altogether powerful
That it burst forth from his being,
Shook off abstraction,
And became tangible form….YOU!

And now, having come forth,
You are brilliant,
Surrounded as you are by divinity and power.
You're here in your totality
And every single inch of space,
Of atmosphere around you
Is filled with Divine Consciousness
Of which you are a part.

Think of the power you must possess
Enveloped as you are by a force complete.
Your strength is God's strength
Is every other being's strength.
Every other being's strength
Is God's strength
Is your strength.

Give; freely give. Take. Be,
And further create.
Well up to your fullest capacity
And burst out again
In Power
In Strength
In Brilliance
In Beauty
And More…and More.

* * *

THOUGHTS TO TAKE AWAY:

You become who you believe you can become

You manifest in your life what you think you deserve

Be consistently aware of your divine nature

Set very high standards for yourself

Don't be afraid to DREAM REALLY BIG DREAMS

Look for opportunities to be of service to others

Life is meant to be joyful; live it that way

Be big on Forgiveness

Express the fullness of your true self

Embrace ALL of life

Choose Happiness

* * *

Dear New You:

Thanks for taking the time to read this book. It is my sincere hope that it will help you to be happy and successful in your endeavors and in your overall life.

Remember the lessons you learned here about values, integrity, and graciousness. These are your beauty marks. They will shine through in everything you do and make you very beautiful indeed, and proud of the person you are. Remember, also, that you are wonderful exactly the way you were born, and hold yourself in high esteem. Be self-confident. Dare to dream the biggest dream you can dream for yourself, and know that the universe will assist you in achieving it.

Finally, be happy. Be a good friend to others, but be your own best friend. This means that you treat yourself well and have all others treat you well. Give respect to yourself and to others; the care and respect you give, you will receive in return. The happiness you create in the universe will surround you always.

Live well.

You have my very best wishes.

Sincerely,
Nordica Francis

20356427R00078

Made in the USA
San Bernardino, CA
08 April 2015